This coloring book belongs to:

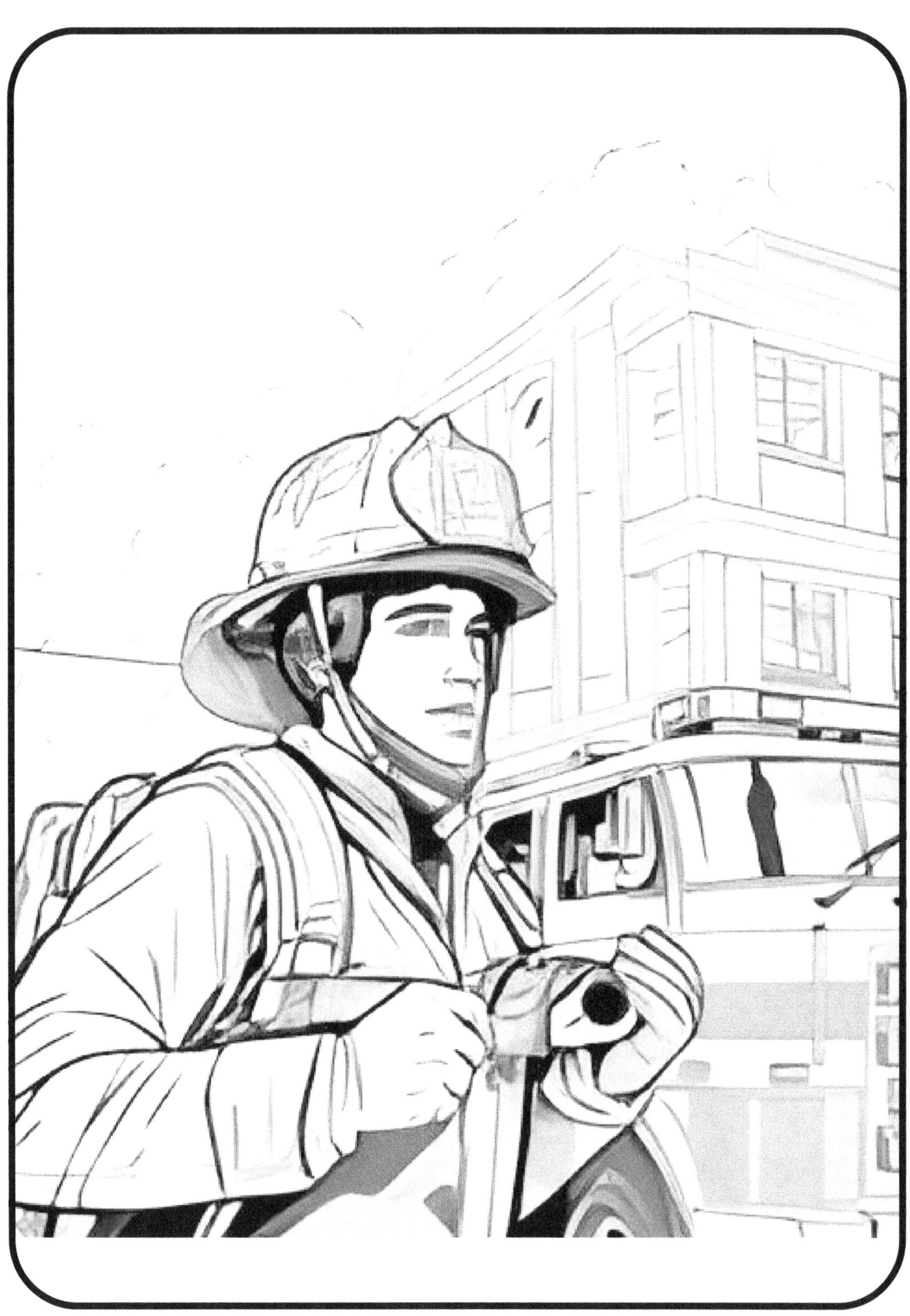

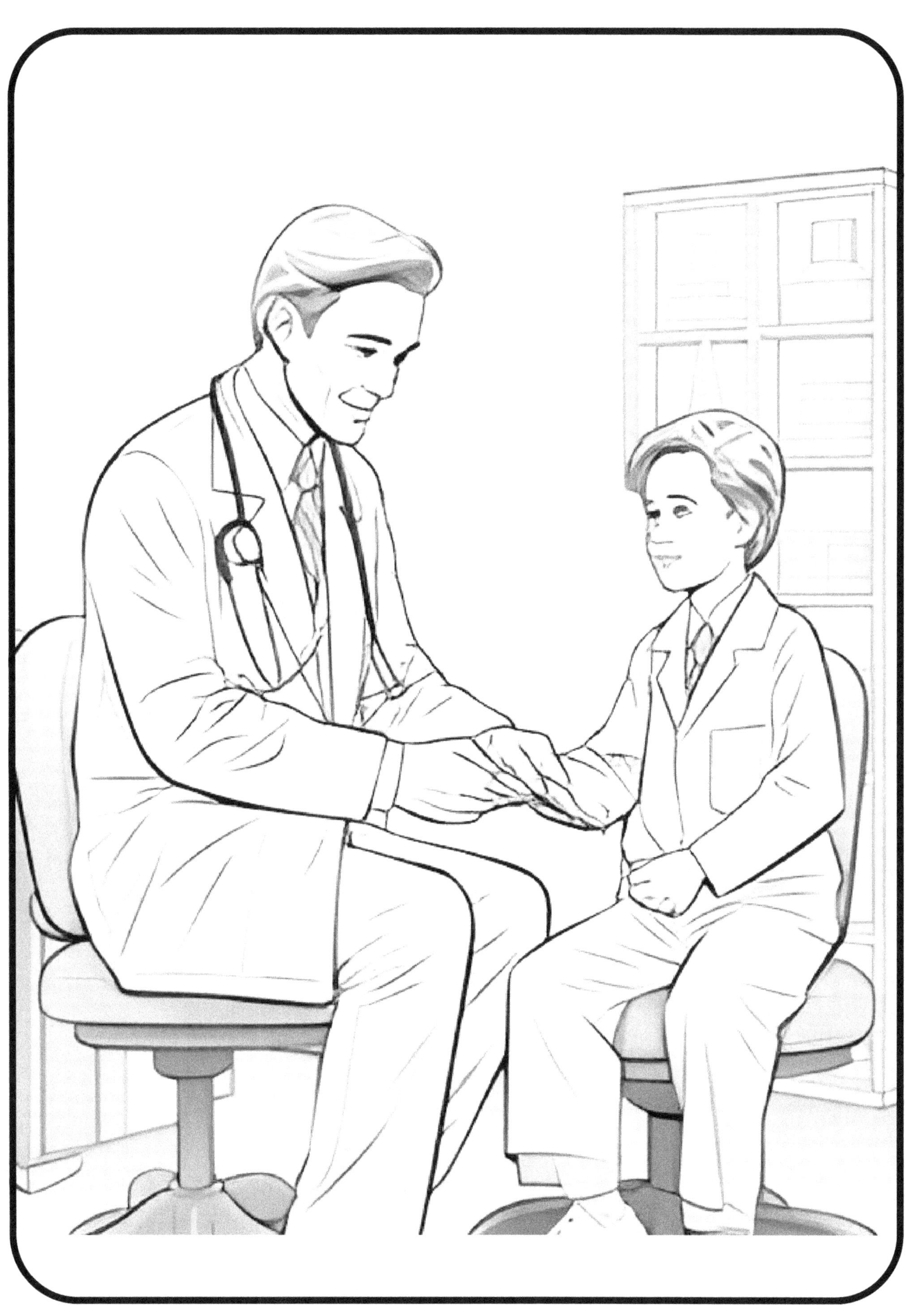

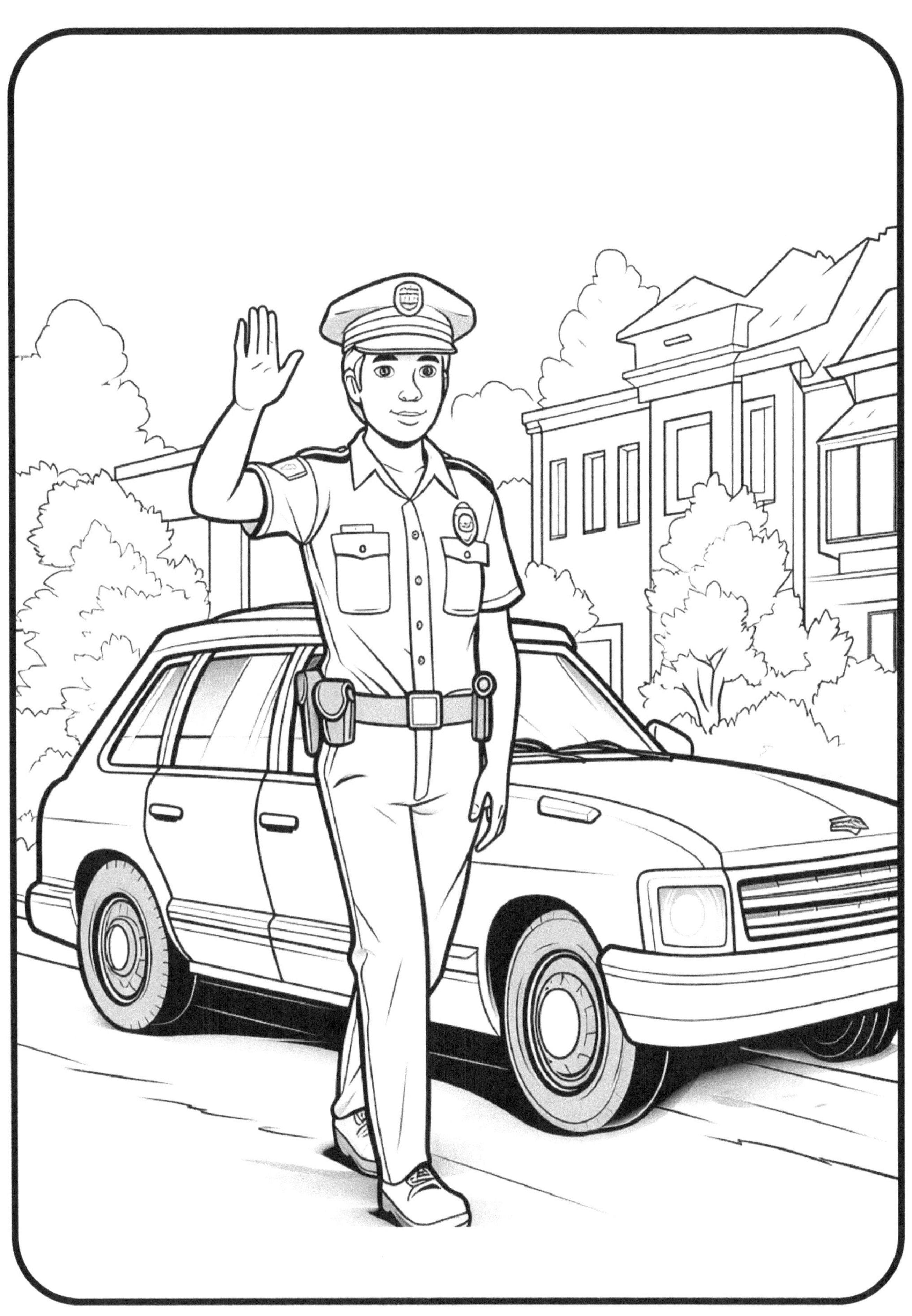

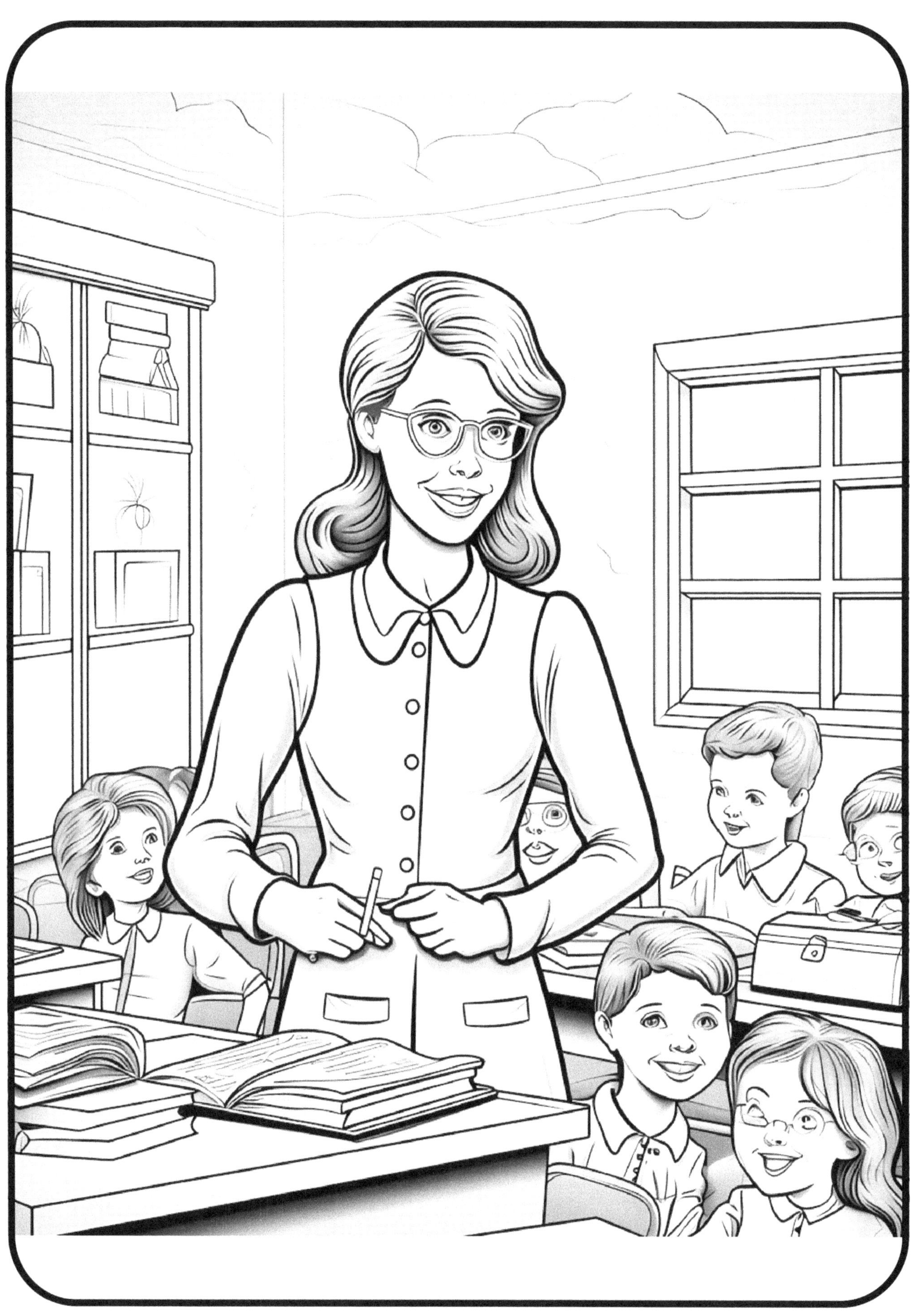

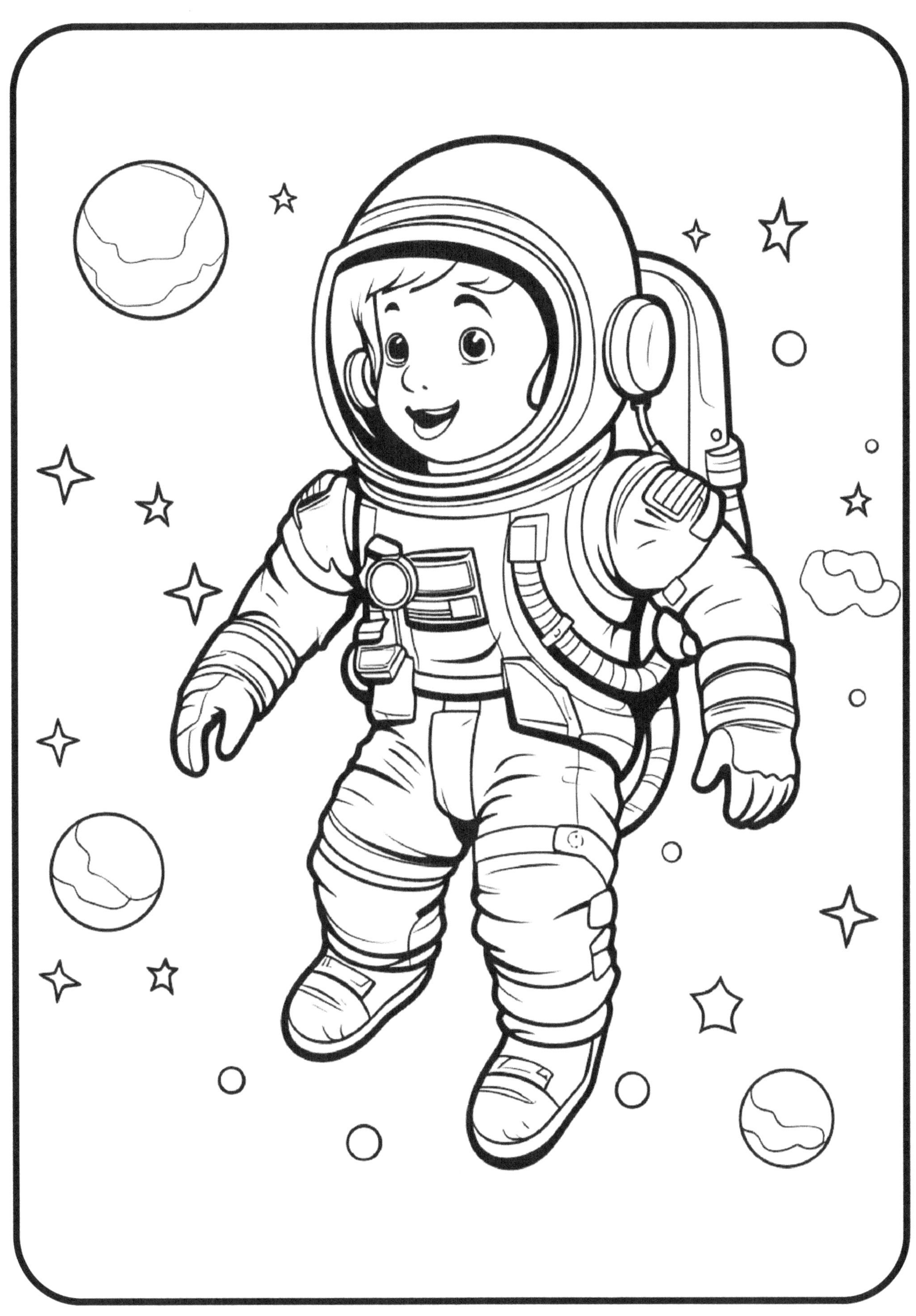

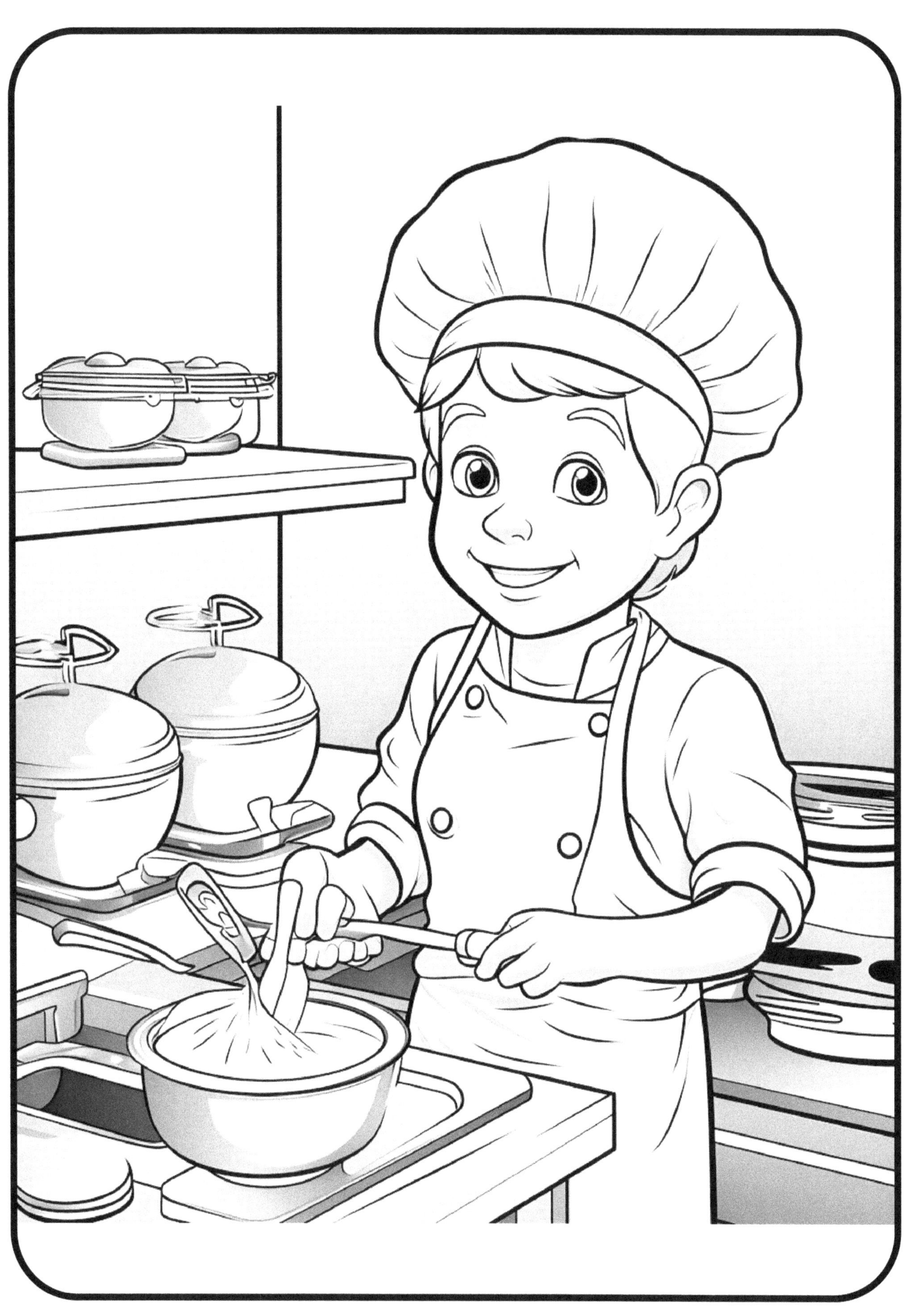

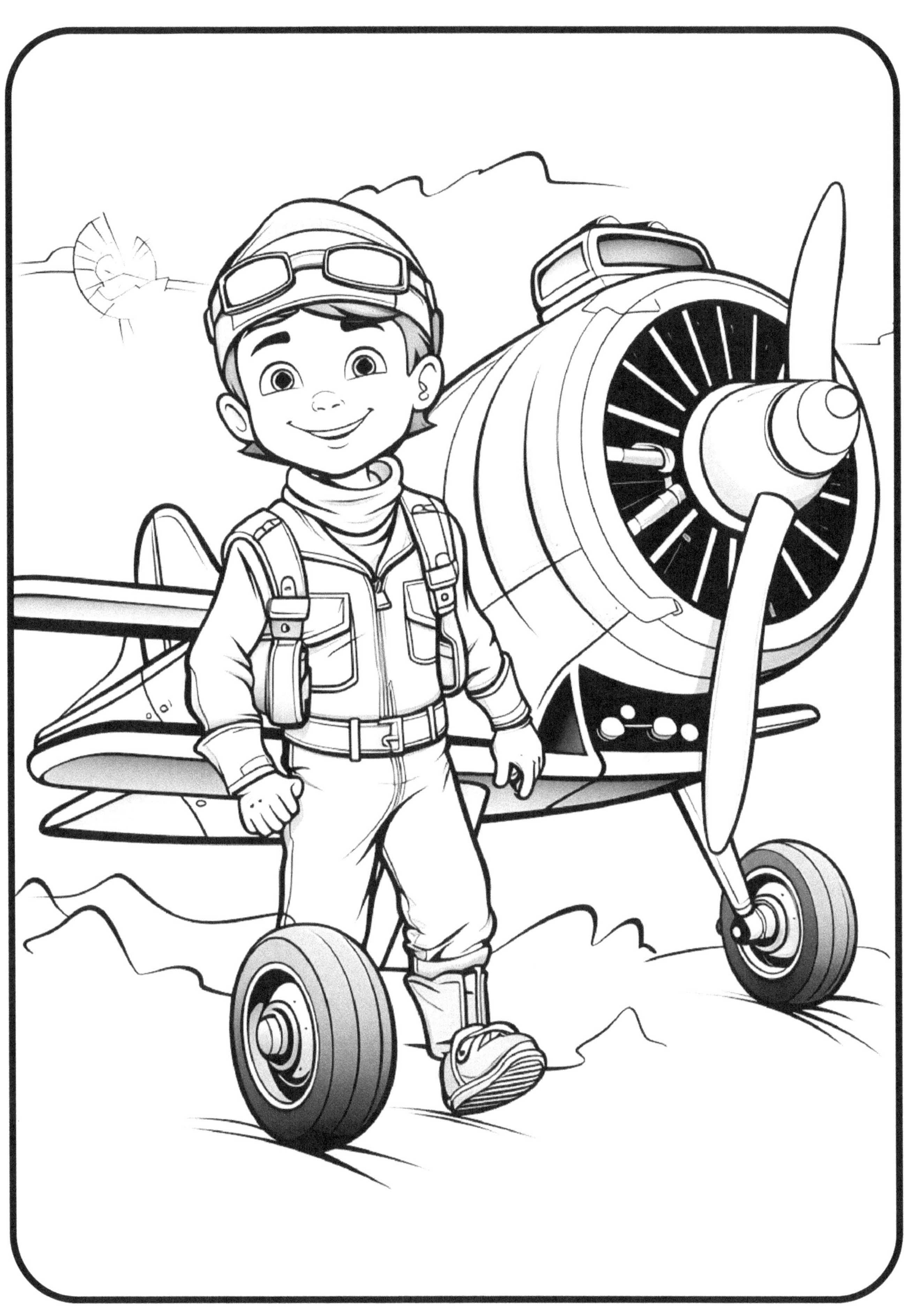

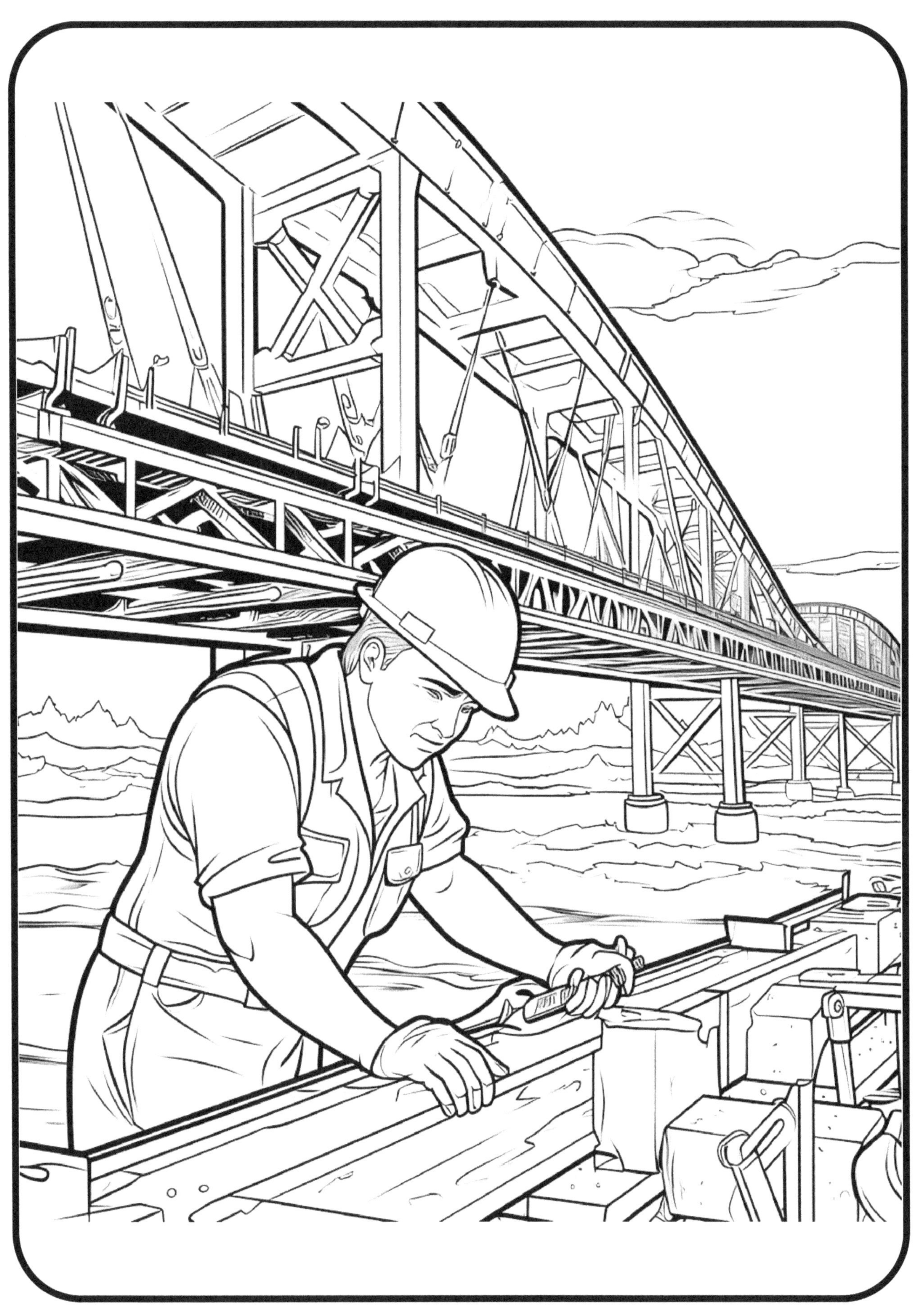

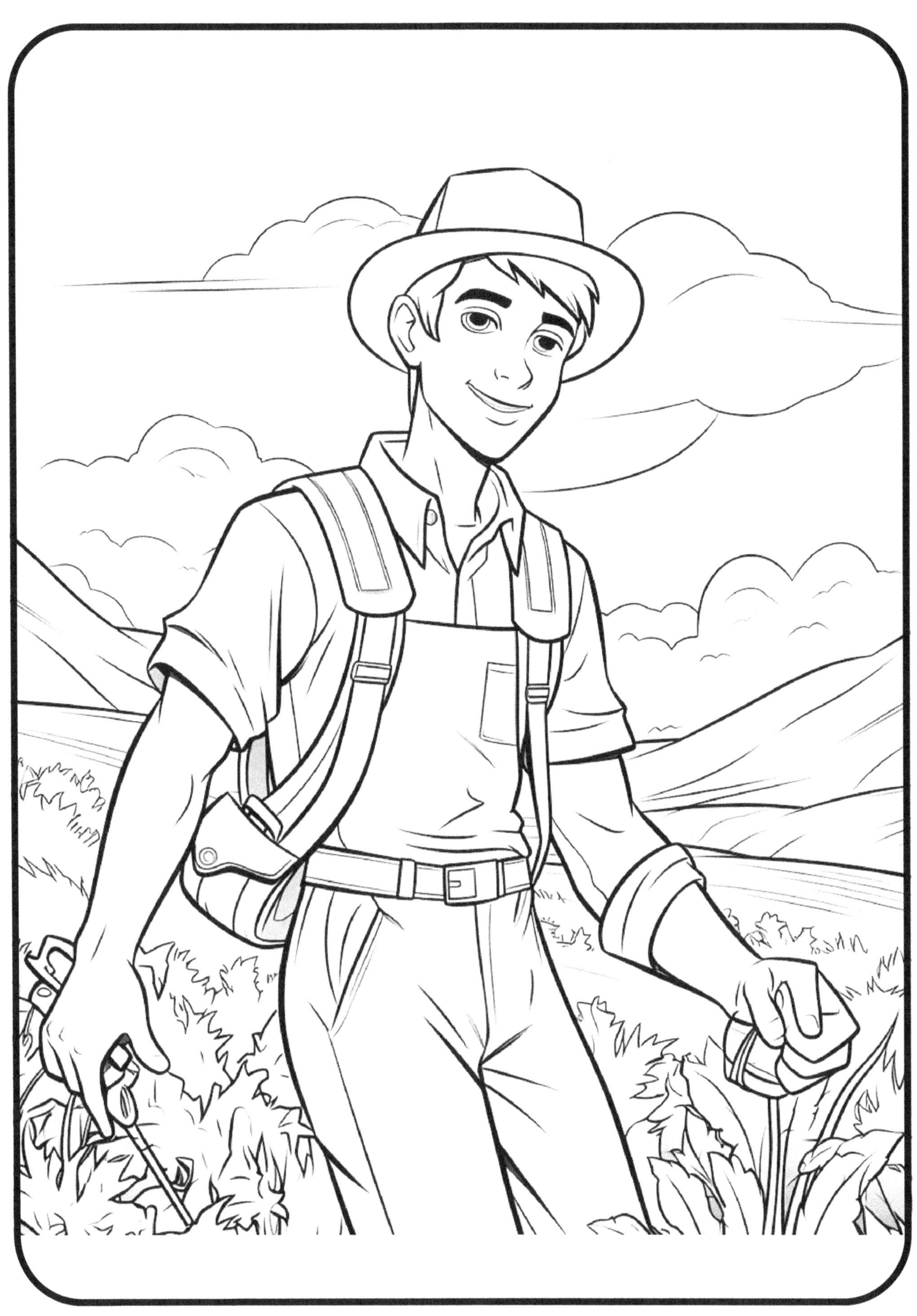

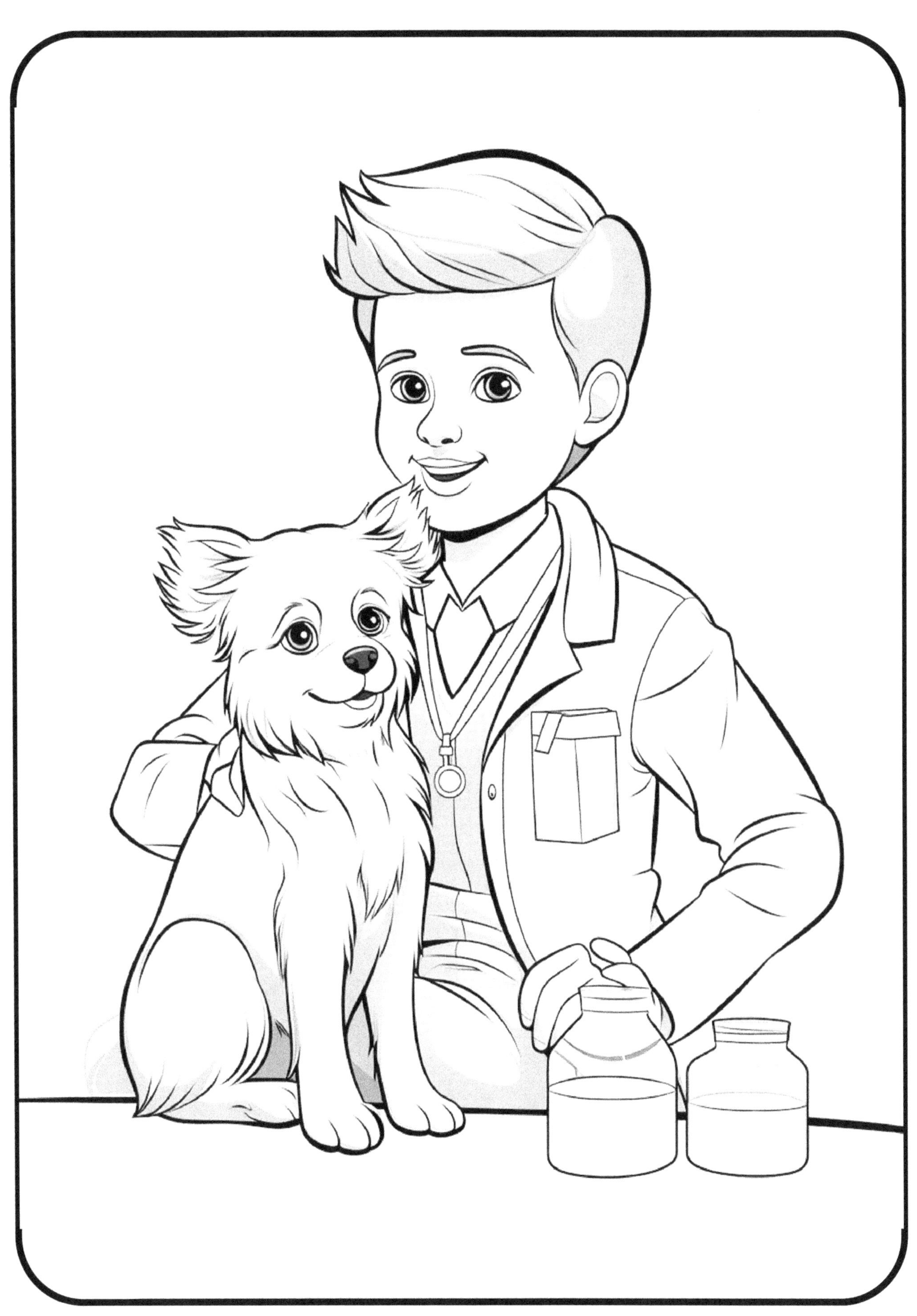

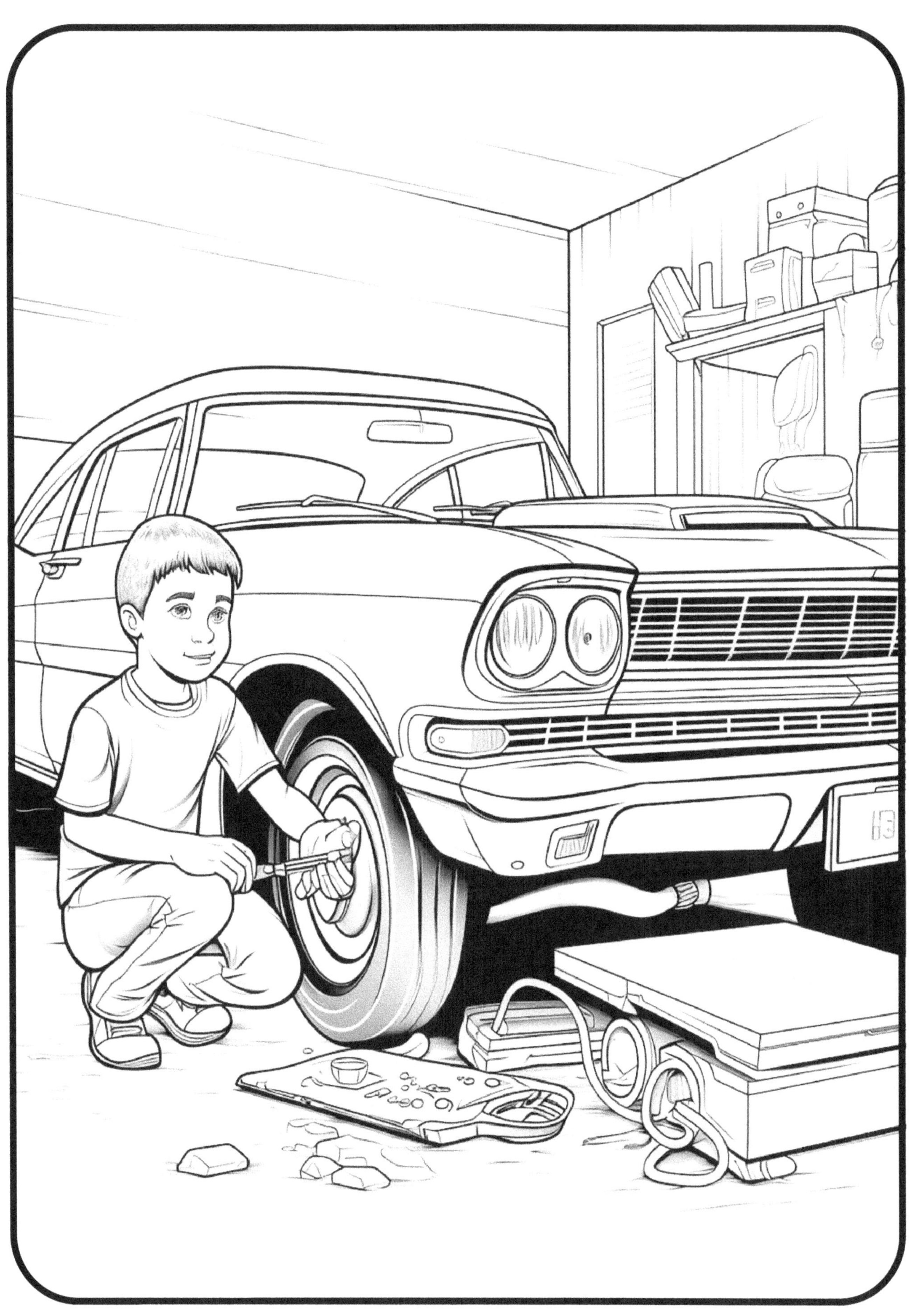

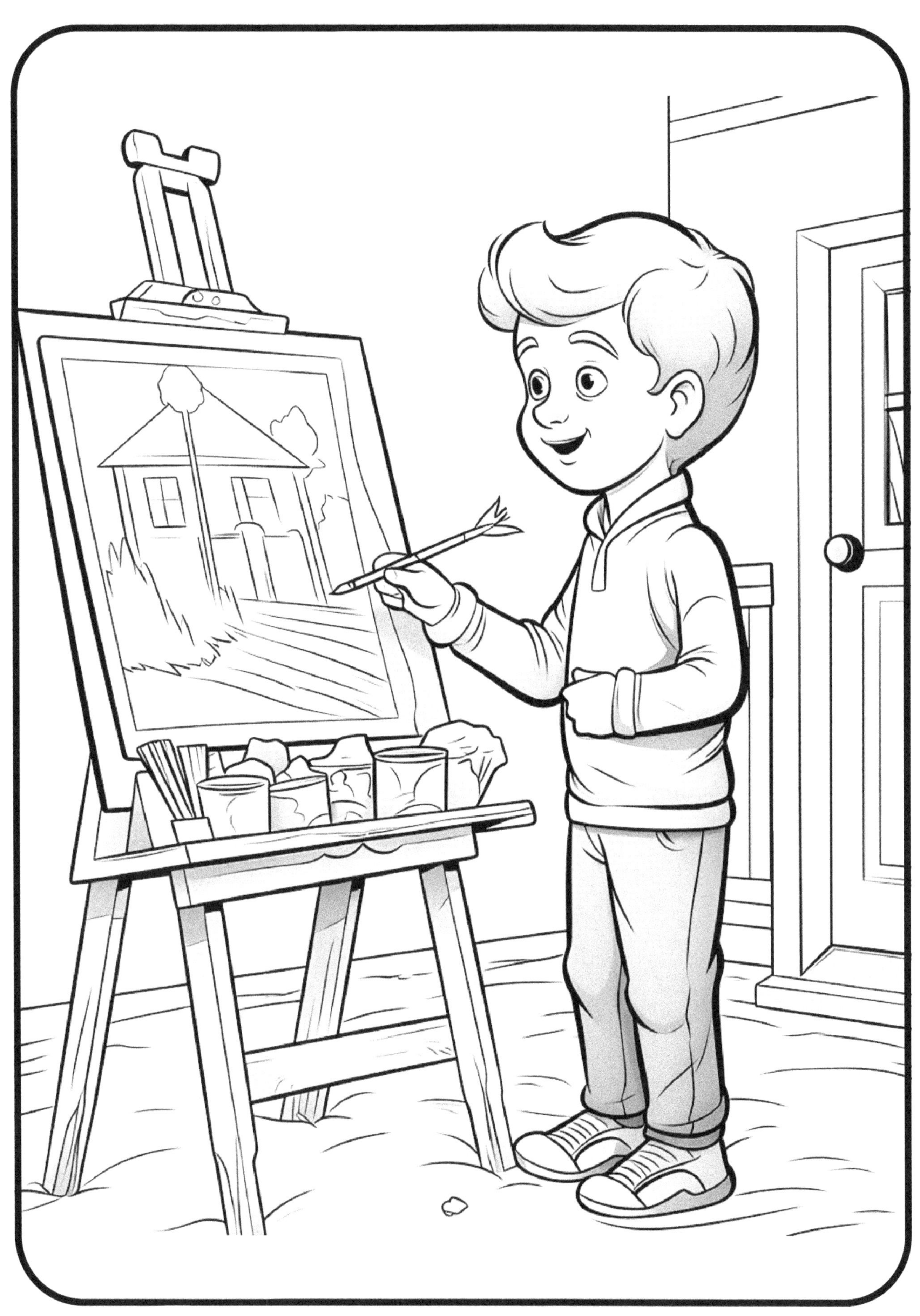

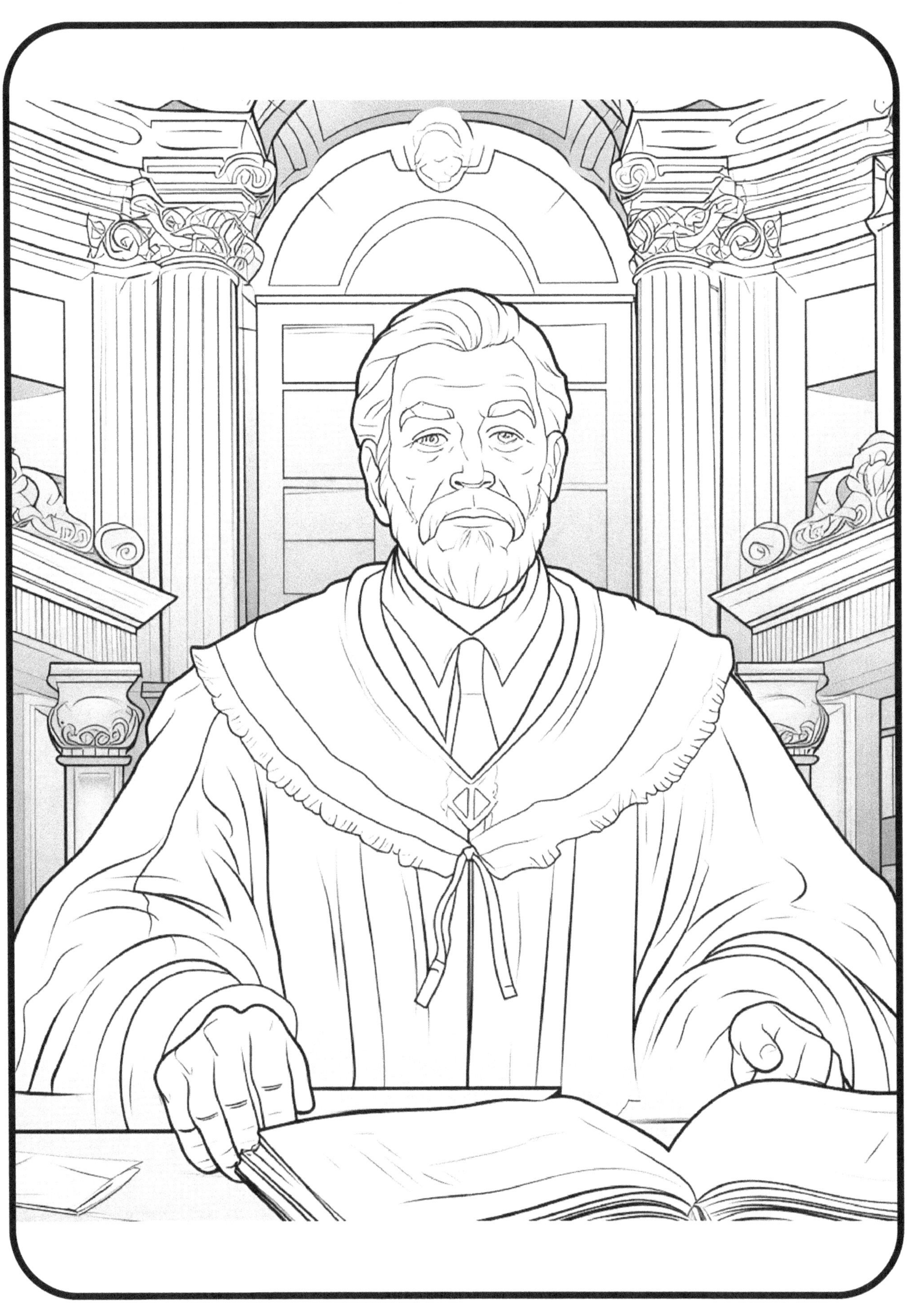

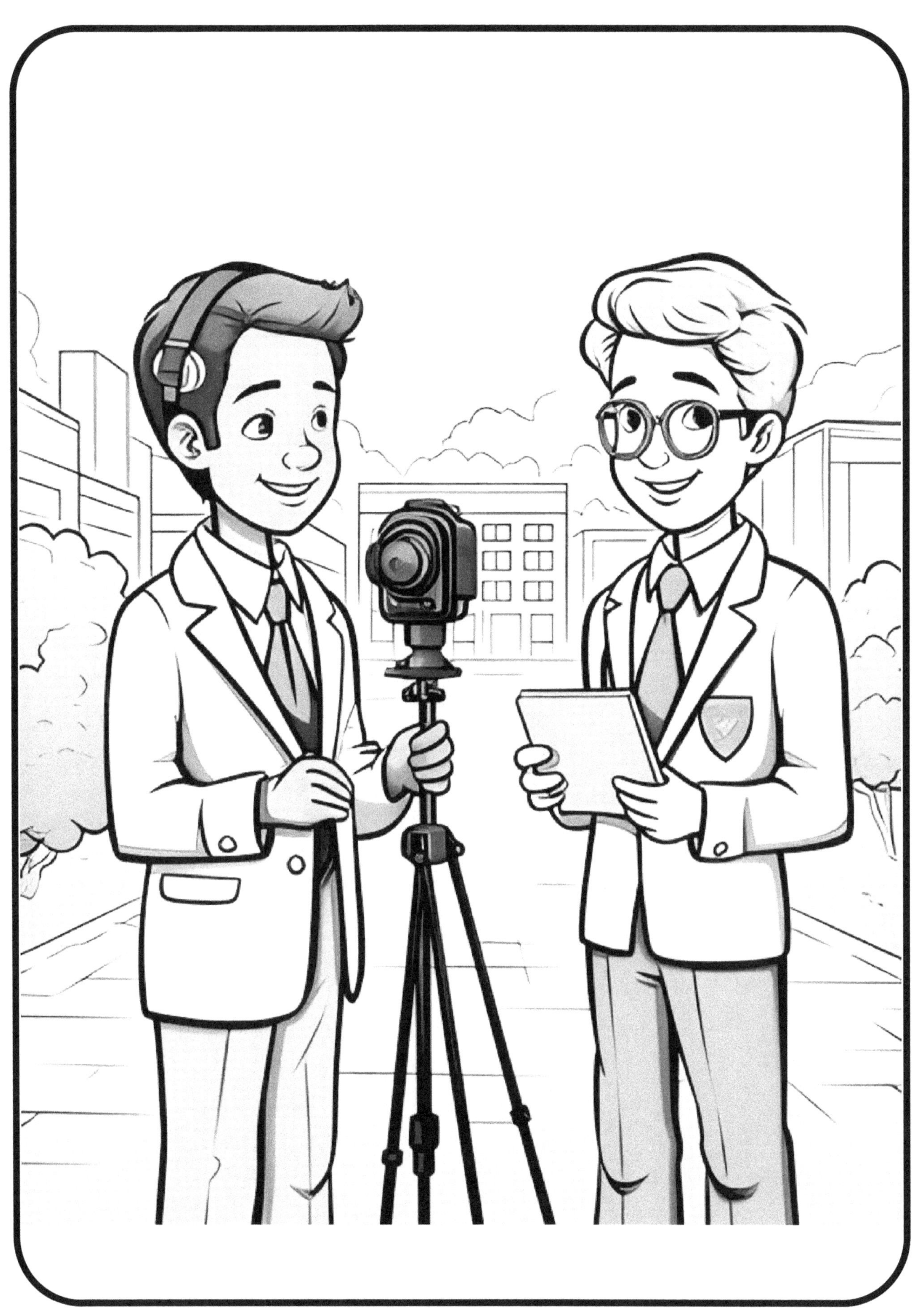

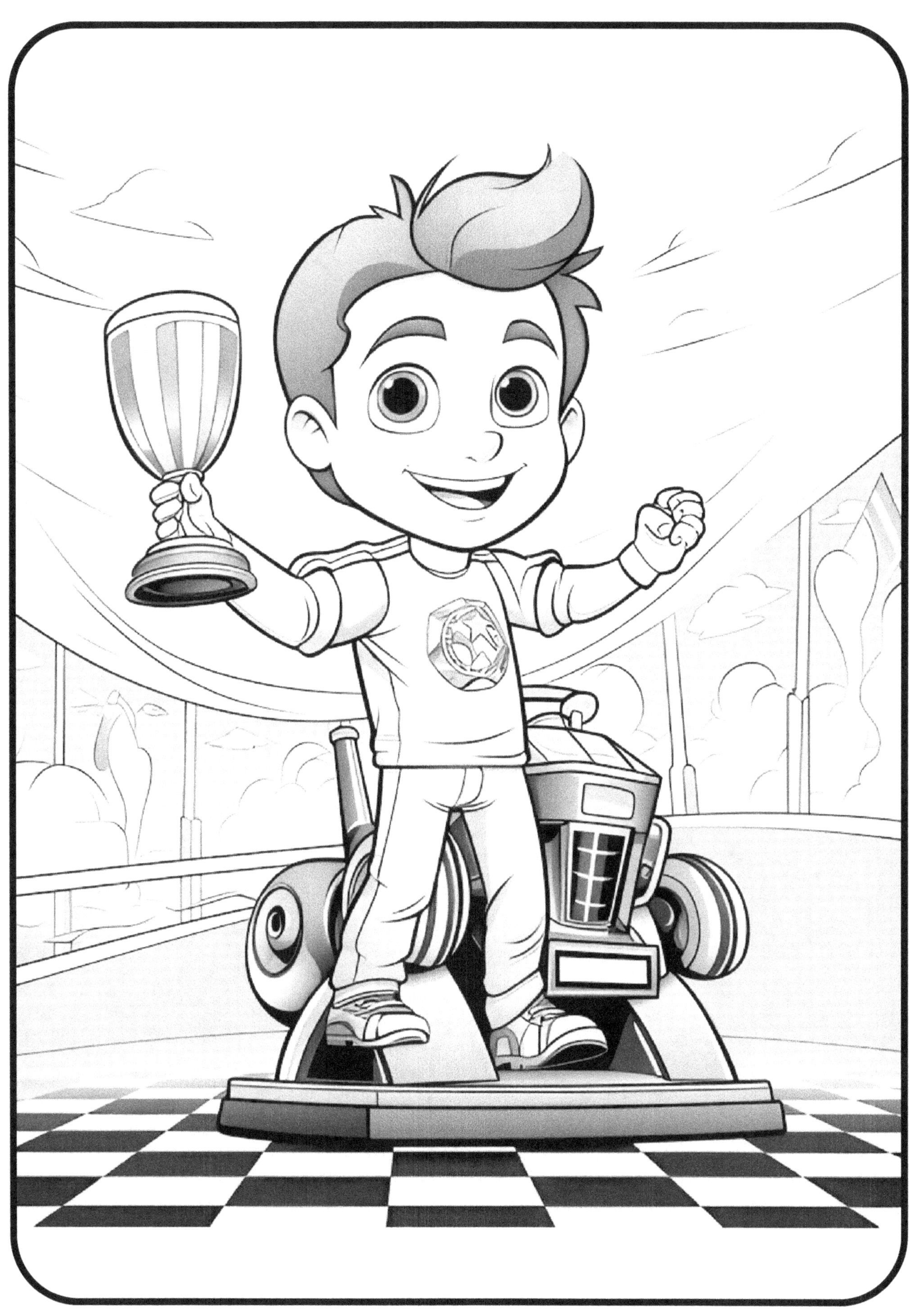

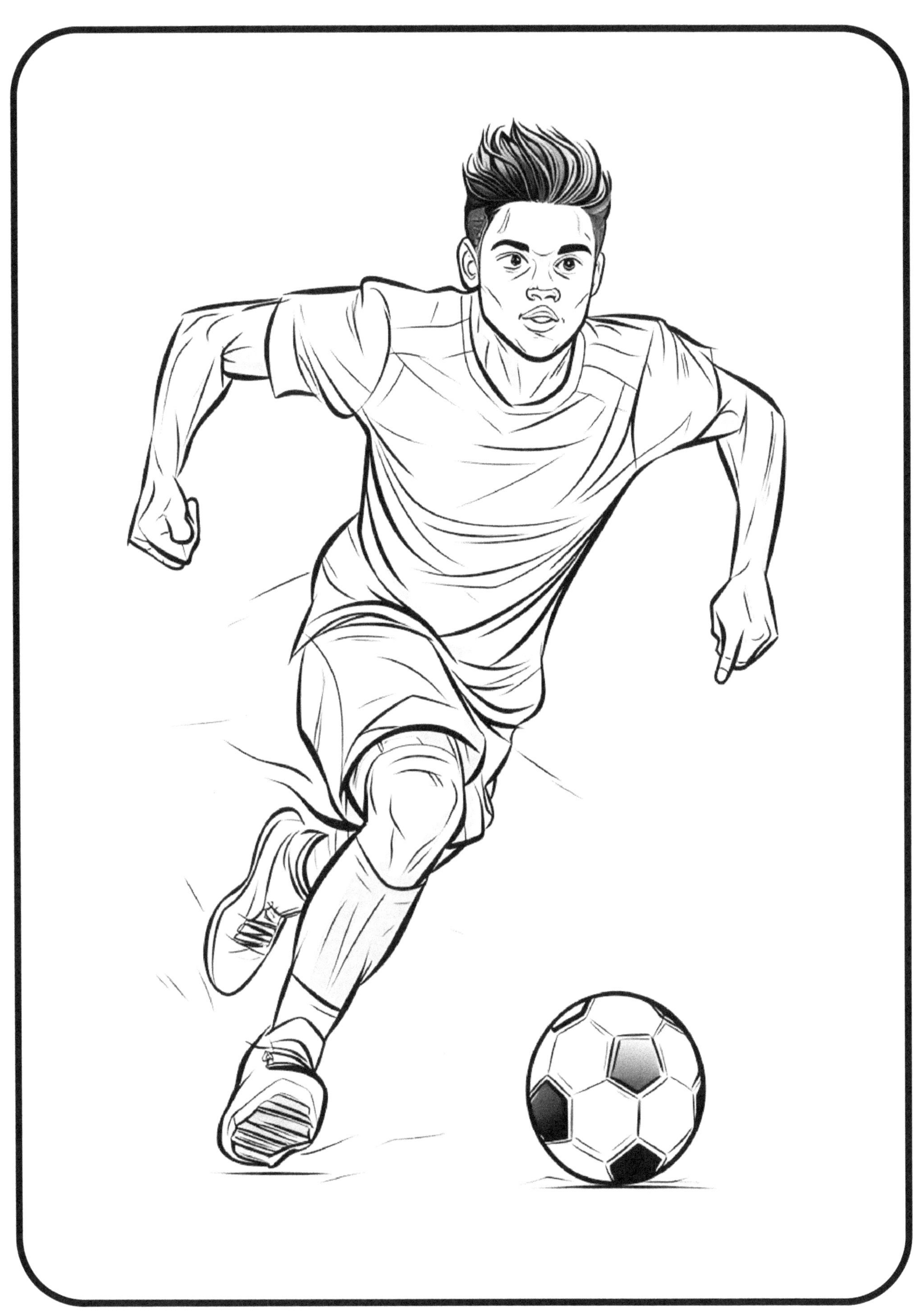

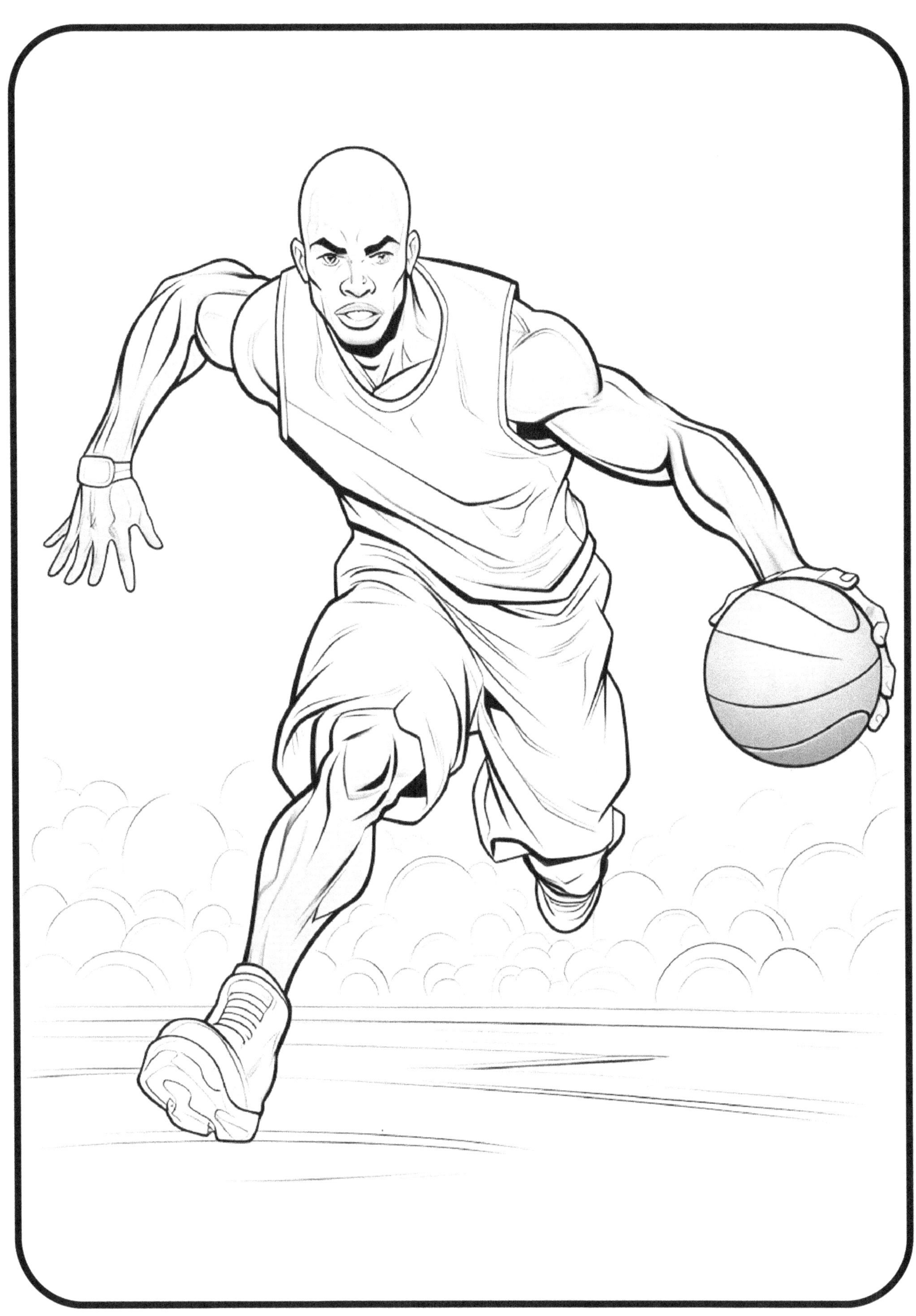

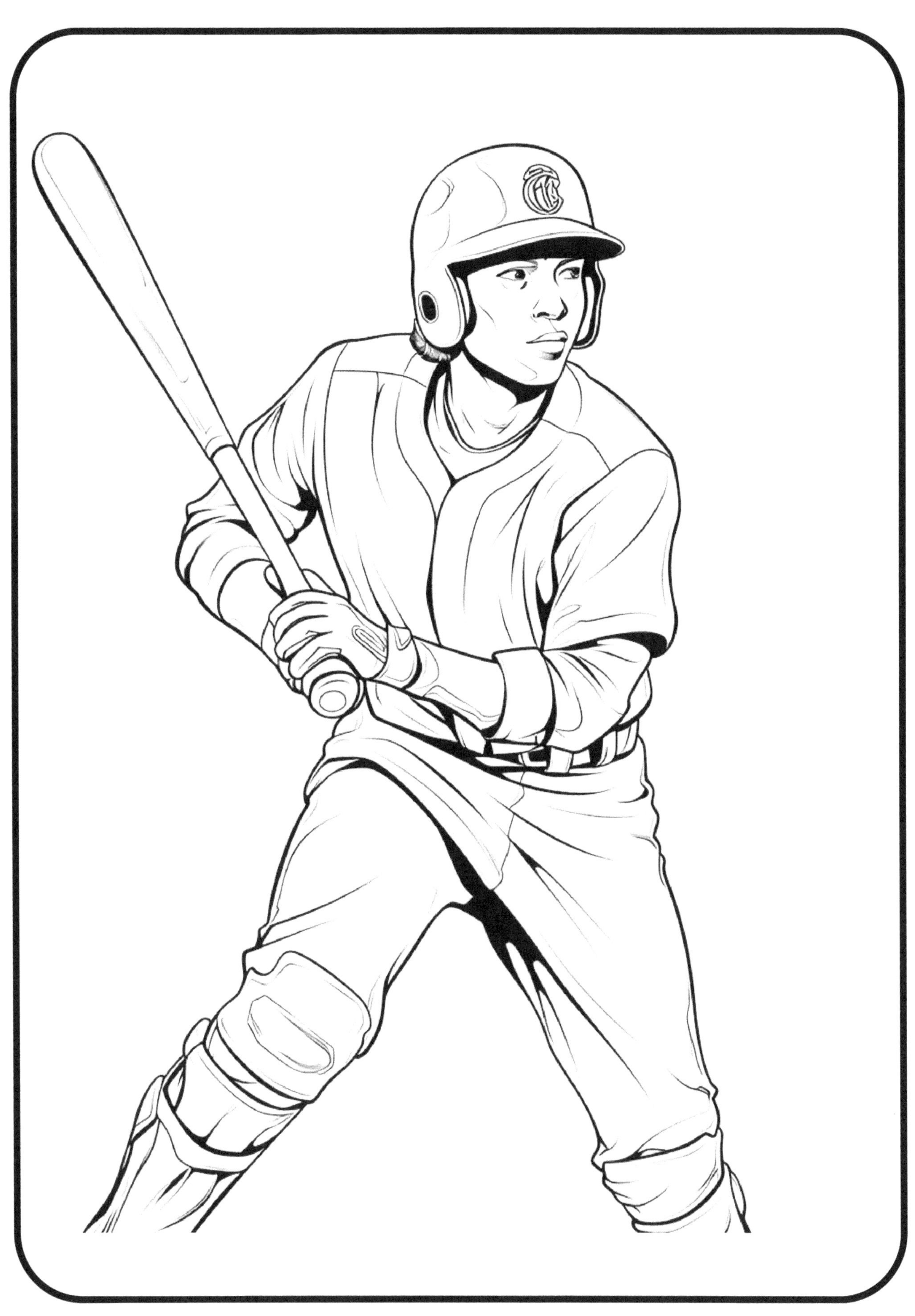

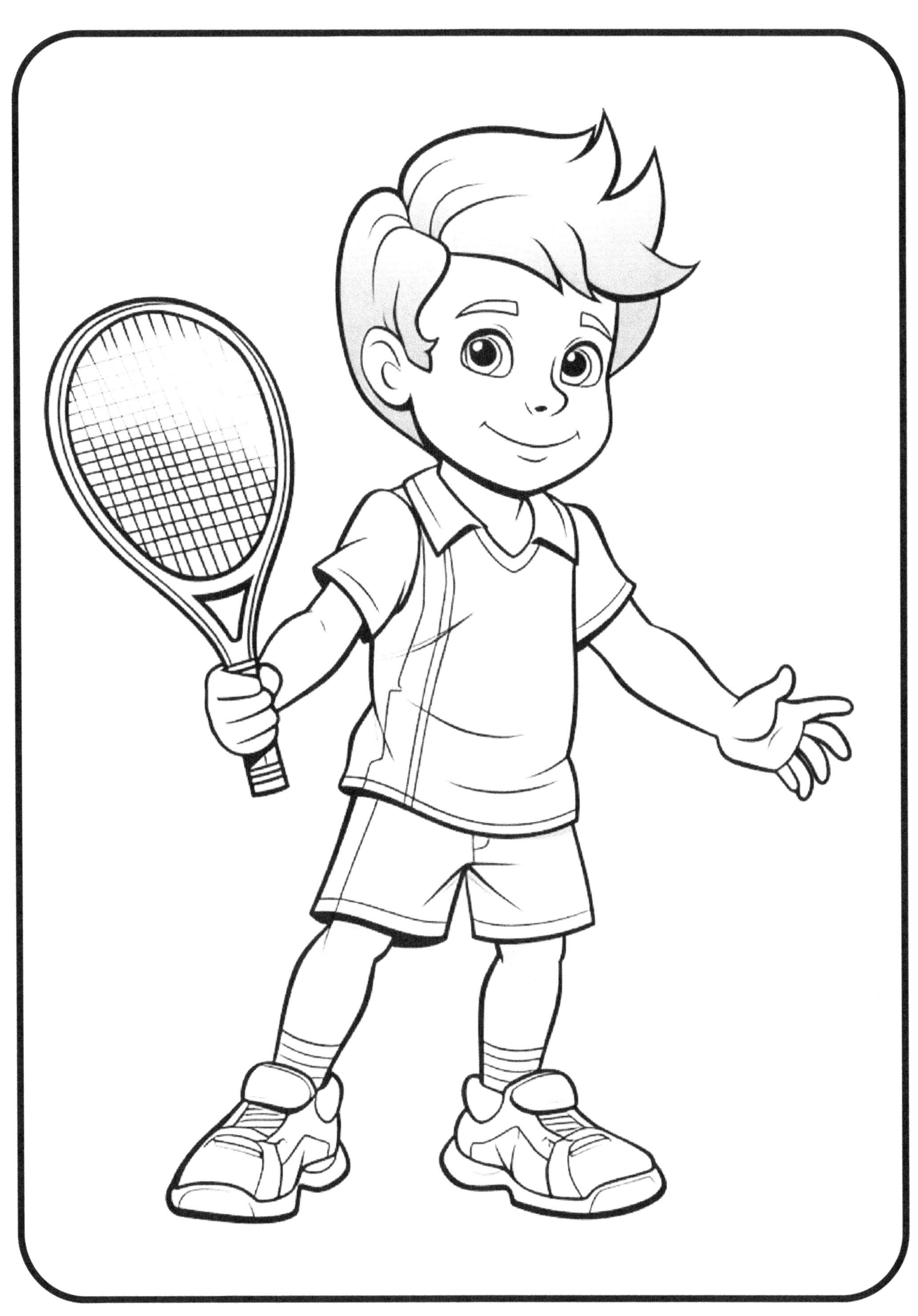

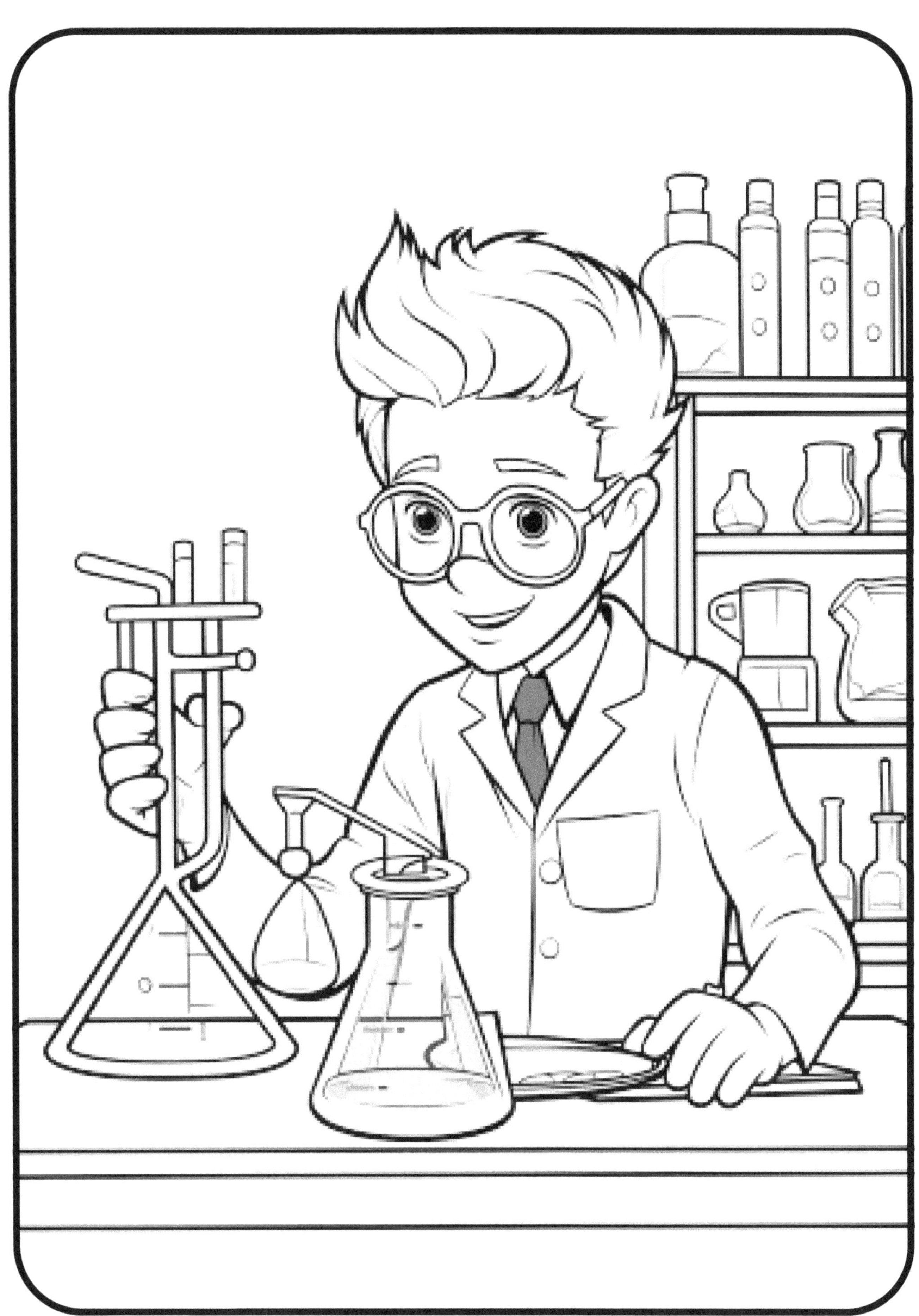

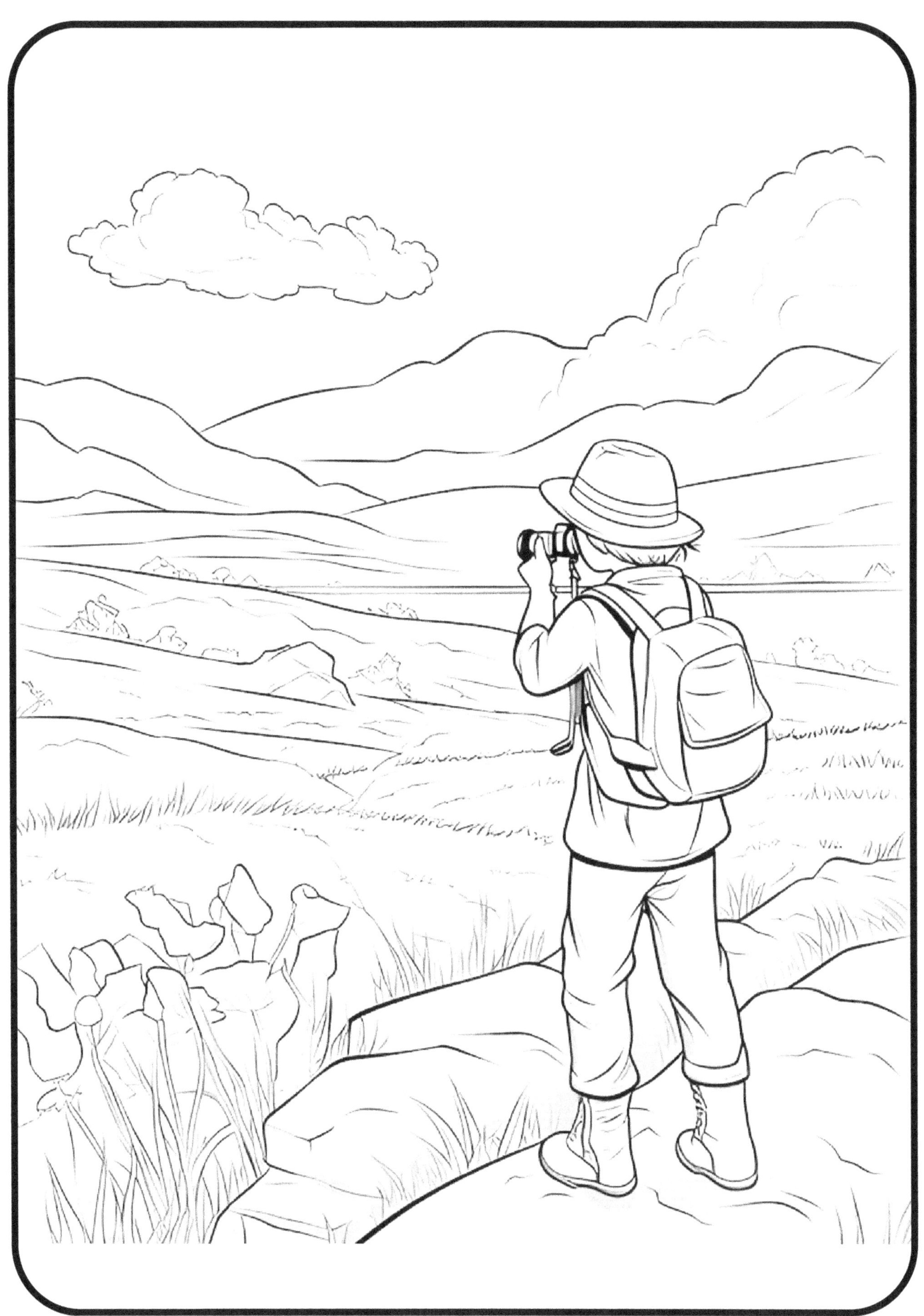

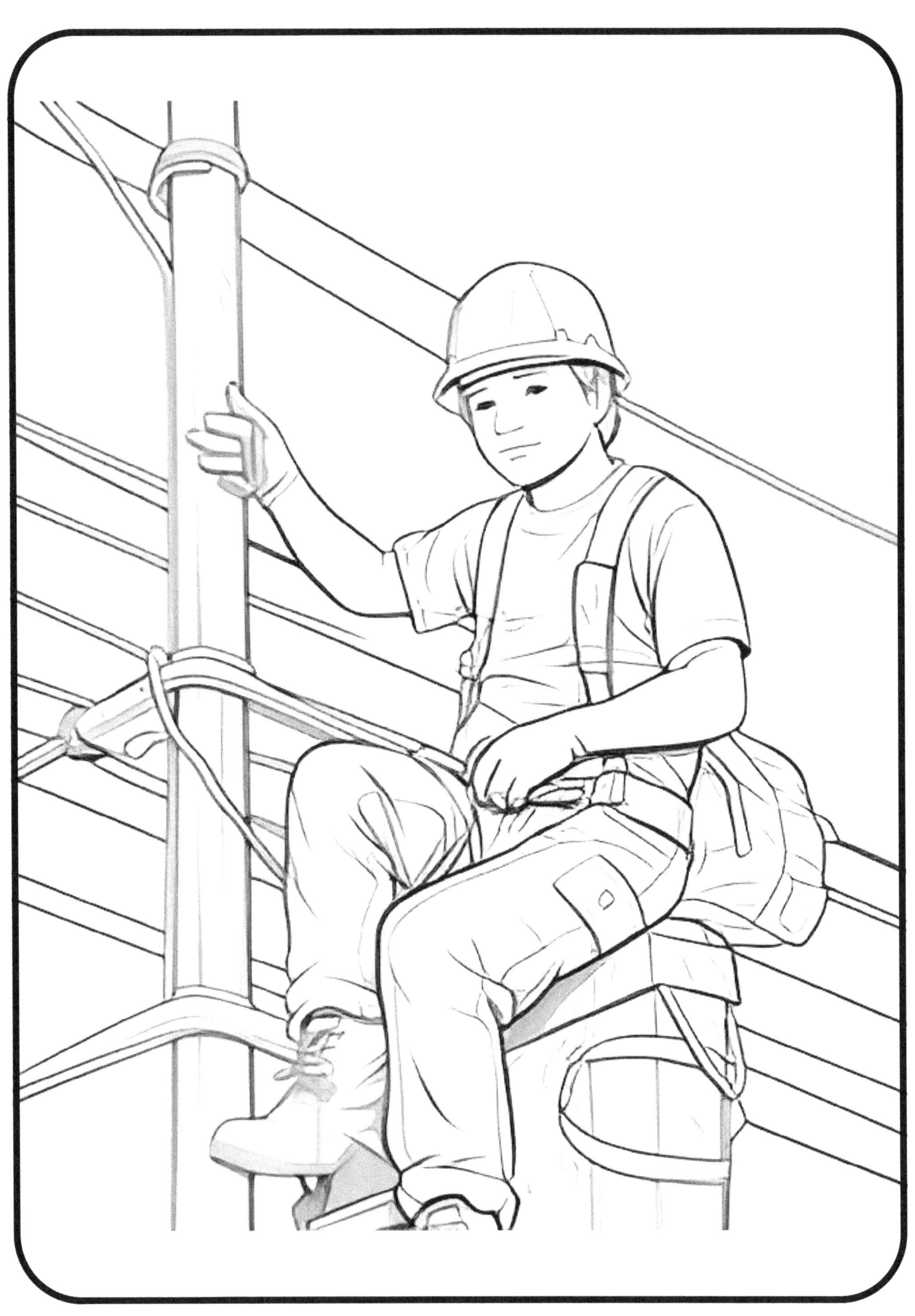

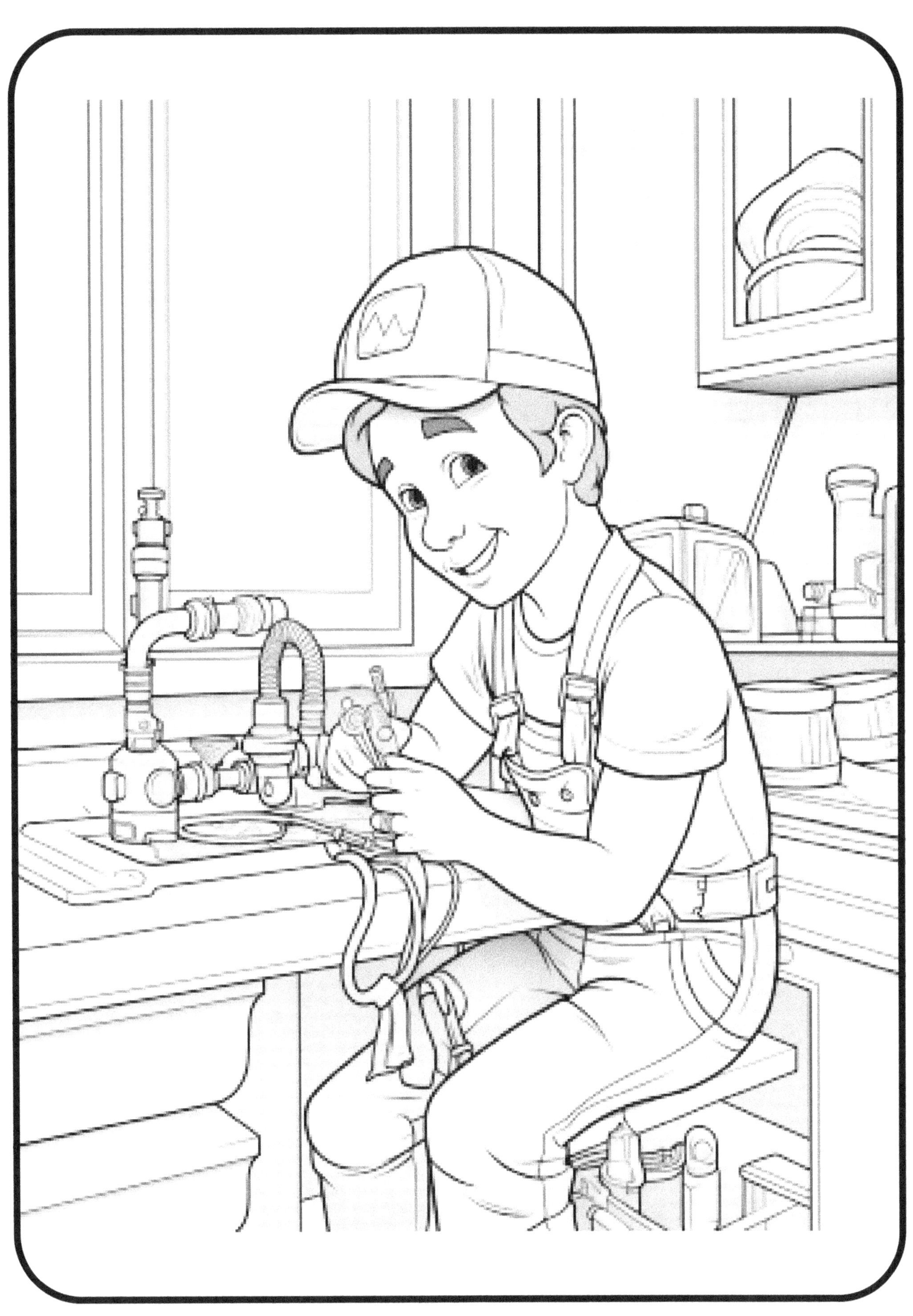

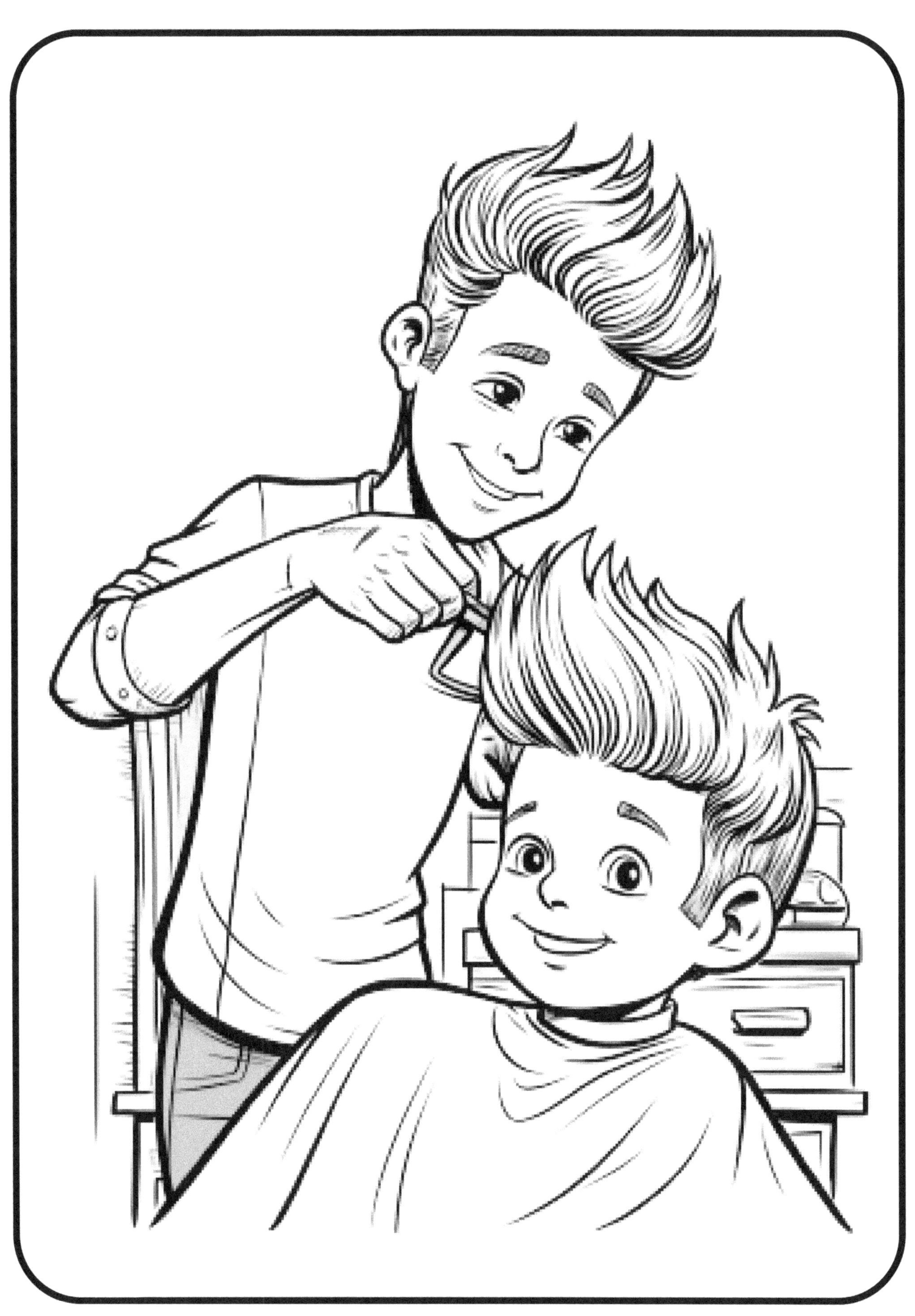

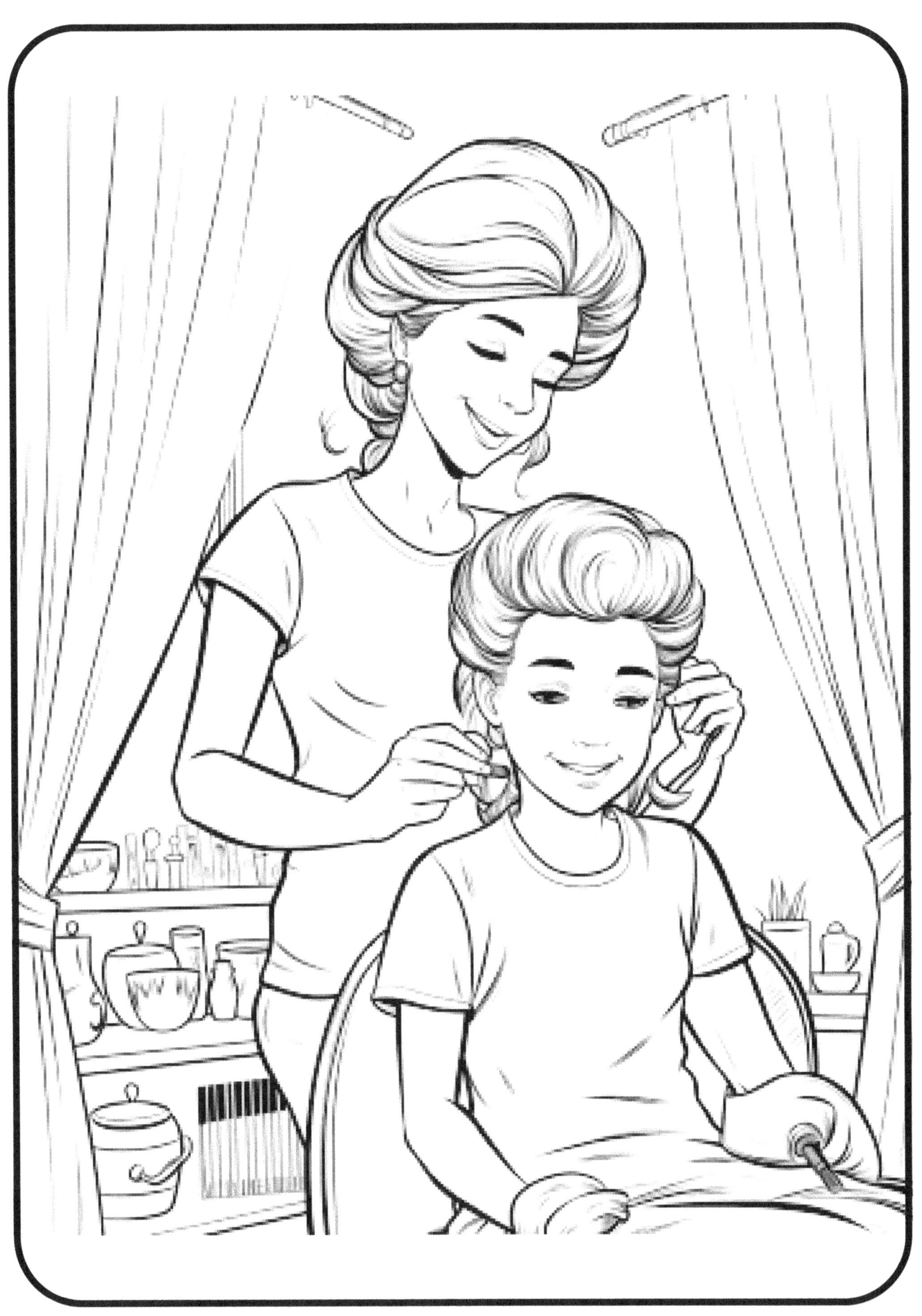

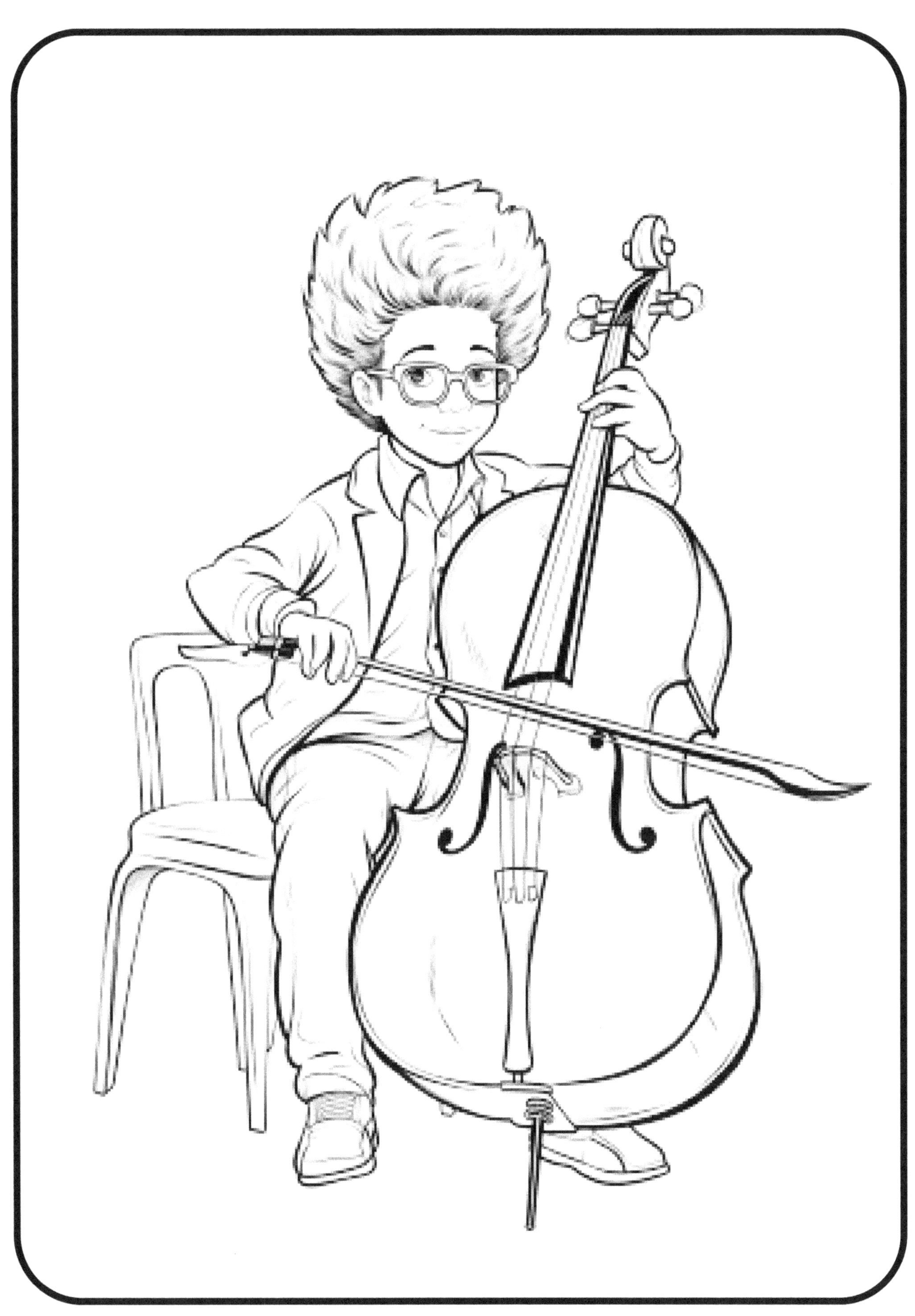

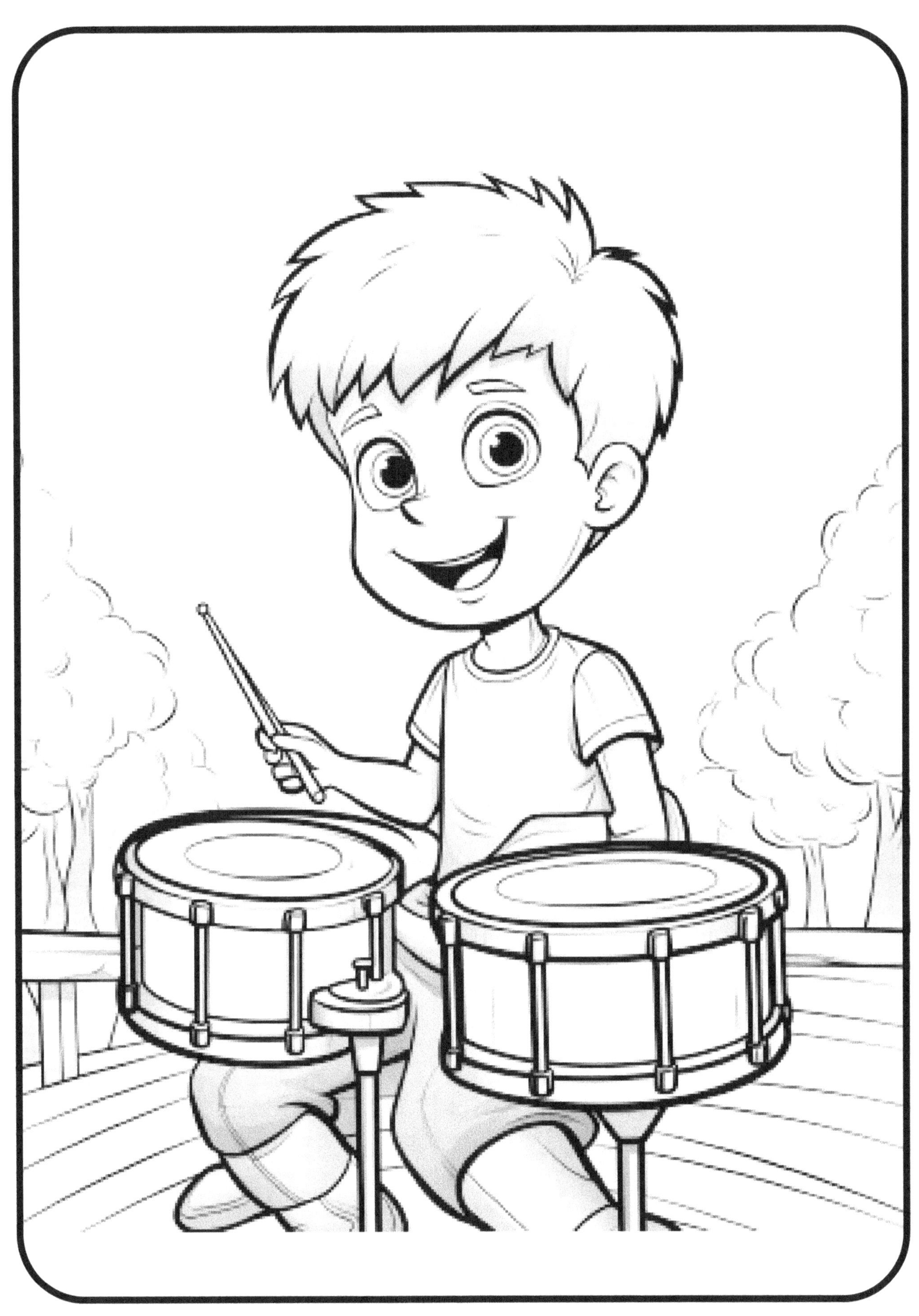

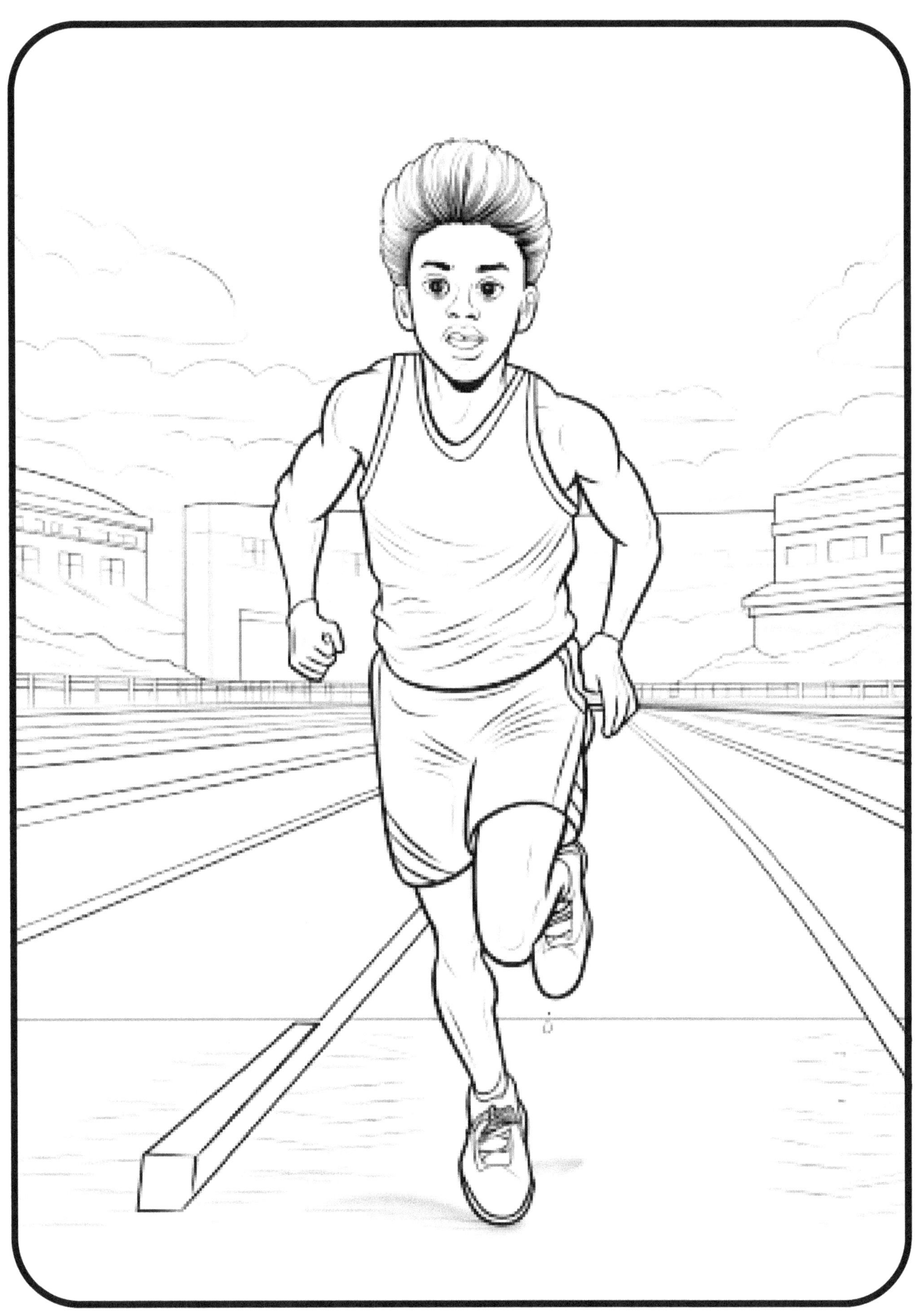

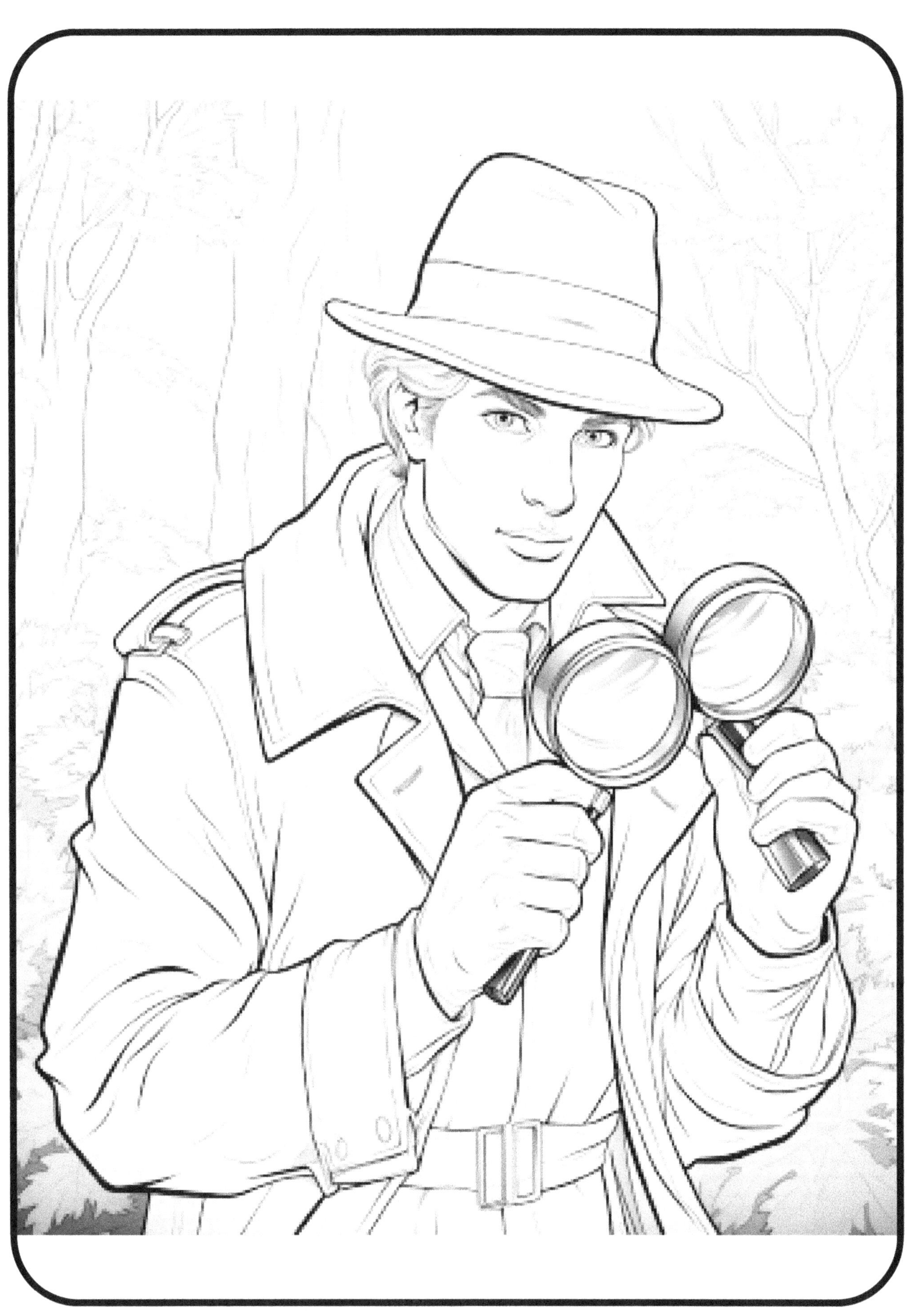

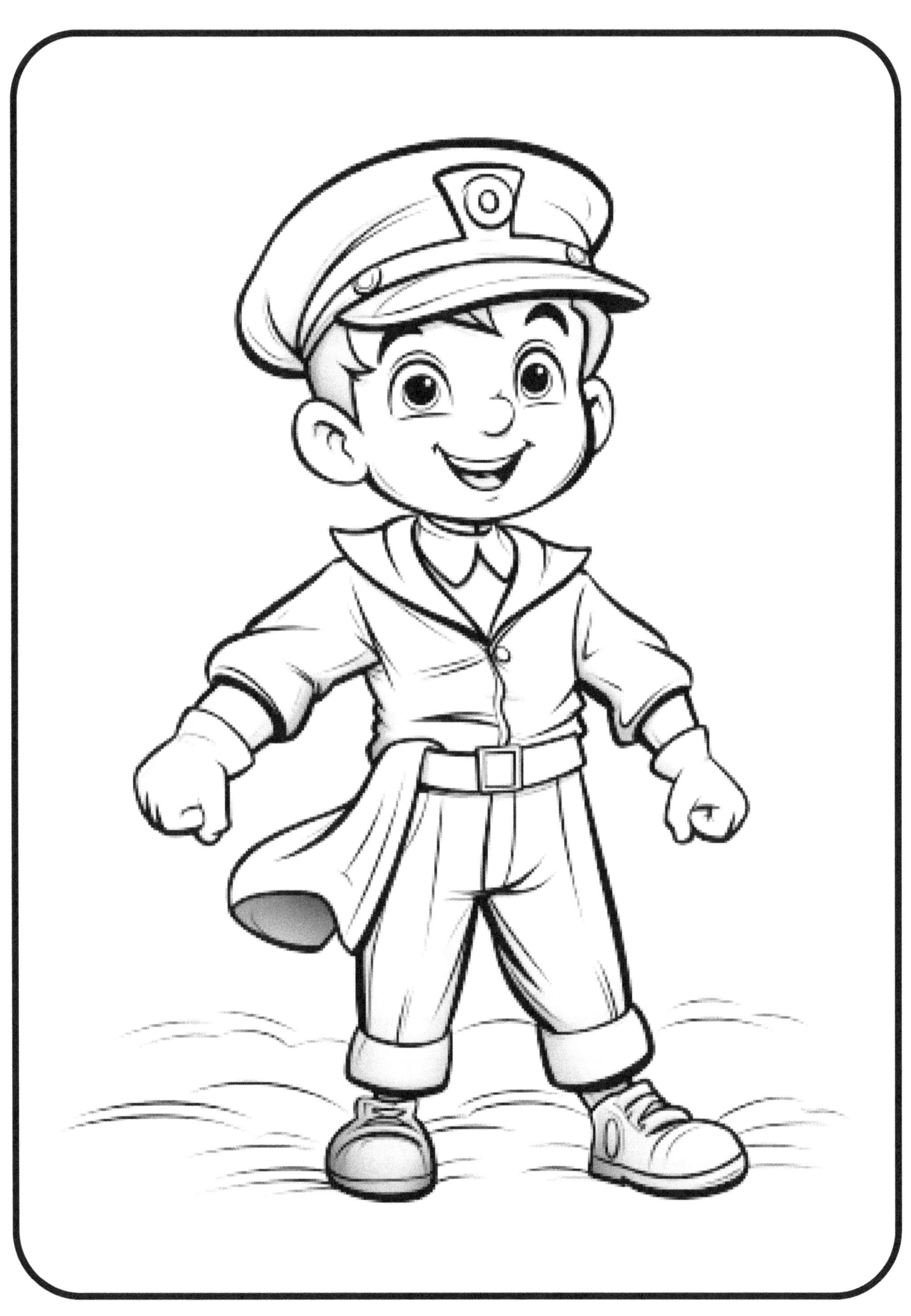